FAMILY

HOMEBUILDERS

COUPLES SERIES

D1054554

BUILDING
YOUR
MARRIAGE

DENNIS RAINEY

PERSONAL STUDY GUIDE

"UNLESS THE LORD BUILDS THE HOUSE
THEY LABOR IN VAIN WHO BUILD IT."
Psalm 127:1

Gospel Light

How to
Let the Lord
Build Your House
and not labor in vain

FamilyLife is a ministry of Campus Crusade for Christ International, an evangelical Christian organization founded in 1951 by Bill Bright. FamilyLife was started in 1976 to help fulfill the Great Commission by strengthening marriages and families and then equipping them to go to the world with the gospel of Jesus Christ. Our FamilyLife Marriage Conference, known as "A Weekend to Remember," is held in most major cities throughout the United States and is one of the fastest-growing marriage conferences in America today. Information on all resources offered by FamilyLife may be obtained by either writing or calling us at the address and telephone number listed below.

■

The HomeBuilders Couples Series: A small-group Bible study dedicated to making your family all that God intended.

Building Your Marriage—Study Guide
ISBN 0-8307-1612-2

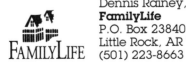

Dennis Rainey, Director
FamilyLife
P.O. Box 23840
Little Rock, AR 72221-3840
(501) 223-8663

A Ministry of Campus Crusade for Christ International
Bill Bright, Founder and President

Published by Gospel Light, Ventura, California 93006

To Jerry and Sheryl Wunder
because your friendship, servanthood, and lives
have made **The HomeBuilders Couples Series** a reality

The HomeBuilders

C O U P L E S   S E R I E S

"Unless the Lord builds the house,
they labor in vain who build it."
Psalm 127:1

CONTENTS

ACKNOWLEDGMENTS

The following Bible study is a result of the vision and labor of a team of individuals committed to strengthening marriages around the world. While I owe many thanks to the entire FamilyLife staff, a few "heroes" deserve special recognition.

First, my friend and colleague Jerry Wunder has been, in many ways, the heart behind this entire project. His unwavering belief in this study has endured months of writing, testing, and final reworking.

Bob Horner played an instrumental role throughout this process through his vital conceptual and content advice. Robert Lewis, Bill McKenzie, and Lee Burrell also made significant contributions toward the content of the Bible study. For help during its earliest stages, I must also thank Mark Dawson and Mike Rutter.

As the study neared completion, a few of our staff emerged as true "champions of the cause." First, there is Julie Denker, whose writer's touch added clarity and definition to my periodic ramblings! And then there are Jeff Lord, who served faithfully as my researcher, and Fred Hitchcock, with his indispensable editing abilities. And finally, there is Donna Guirard and her finishing touches on the "look" and design of the series.

Julie and Jeff also spent many hours at the word processor entering the seemingly endless revisions. Tim Allen and Brenda Harris also were a help in the final stages with word processing. As always, Jeff Tikson pitched in, especially when I became ill, and pushed the study through to the end.

Don and Sally Meredith have also influenced our ministry and our lives in so many ways and, as a result, leave a legacy through this study.

There were many groups—around the country—who participated in pilot home studies. Thanks for your feedback. It was invaluable.

And last, I need to extend a heartfelt word of appreciation to Wes Haystead. Thank you, Wes, for coming alongside of our team and helping to make this dream a reality.

How to
Let the Lord
Build Your House

and not labor in vain

INTRODUCTION

What Is The HomeBuilders Couples Series?

Do you remember the first time you fell in love? That junior high— or elementary school—"crush" stirred your affections with little or no effort on your part. We use the term "falling in love" to describe the phenomenon of suddenly discovering our emotions have been captured by someone delightful.

Unfortunately, our society tends to make us think that all loving relationships should be equally as effortless. Thus, millions of couples, Christians included, approach their marriage certain that the emotions they feel will carry them through any difficulties. And millions of couples quickly learn that a good marriage does not automatically happen.

Otherwise intelligent people, who would not think of buying a car, investing money, or even going to the grocery store without some initial planning, enter into marriage with no plan of how to make their marriage succeed.

But God has already provided the plan, a set of blueprints for a truly godly marriage. His plan is designed to enable two people to grow together in a mutually satisfying relationship, and then to look beyond their own marriage to others. Ignoring this plan leads to isolation and separation between husband and wife—the pattern so evident in the majority of homes today. Even when great energy is expended, failure to follow God's blueprints results in wasted effort, bitter disappointment —and, in far too many cases, divorce.

In response to this need in marriages today, FamilyLife of Campus Crusade for Christ is developing a series of small-group Bible studies called **The HomeBuilders Couples Series.** This series is designed to answer one question for couples:

How Do You Build a Distinctively Christian Marriage?

It is our hope that in answering this question with the biblical blueprints for building a home, we will see the development of growing, thriving marriages filled with the love of Christ.

FamilyLife of Campus Crusade for Christ is committed to strengthening your family. We hope **The HomeBuilders Couples Series** will equip you as a couple to build a truly godly home.

This introductory study, **Building Your Marriage,** is designed to provide the basis upon which a godly marriage can be built. It is composed of seven sessions, each built around a concept that will enrich your marriage in the weeks that follow.

The Bible: Your Blueprints for a Godly Marriage

> The Bible is alive, it speaks to me;
> it has feet, it runs after me;
> it has hands, it lays its hold on me.
>
> Martin Luther

You will notice as you proceed through this study that the Bible is referred to frequently as the final authority on the issues of life and marriage. Although written centuries ago, this Book still speaks clearly and powerfully to the conflicts and struggles faced by men and women. The Bible is God's Word, His blueprints for building a godly home and for dealing with the practical issues of living.

While the Scripture has only one primary interpretation, there may be several appropriate applications. Some of the Scriptures used in this series were not originally written with marriage in mind, but they can be applied practically to the husband-wife relationship.

We encourage you to have a Bible with you for each session. The *New American Standard Bible* and the *New International Version* are two excellent English translations which make the Bible easy to understand.

Ground Rules for These Sessions

These sessions are designed to be enjoyable and informative—and nonthreatening. Three simple ground rules will help insure that you feel comfortable and that everyone gets the most out of the series:

1. Share nothing about your marriage that will embarrass your mate.

2. You may pass on any question you do not want to answer.

3. Each time between sessions, complete the **HomeBuilders Project** (a few questions for you and your mate to discuss). Then be prepared to share one result at the next group meeting.

Resources

Familylife recommends these outstanding aids to maximize your **HomeBuilders** study experience:

1. If doing this as a couple, we would recommend one Study Guide for each spouse. The Leader's Guide would also be very beneficial.

2. Listen to the tape series, **Oneness: God's Design for Marriage**.

3. If you have been to the FamilyLife Marriage Conference, you will find the **FamilyLife Marriage Conference Manual** to be a useful tool as you go through **The HomeBuilders Couples Series.**

4. Your best resource is one another—others can help us maximize our lives as we learn to be accountable for our actions and lives. Be accountable to one another and to another couple for the session and projects completion.

H O M E B U I L D E R S
P R I N C I P L E S

HomeBuilders Principle #1: It is only as you yield and submit your life to God, obey His Word, and deny yourself that you can experience intimacy and build a godly marriage.

HomeBuilders Principle #2: Oneness in marriage involves complete unity with each other.

HomeBuilders Principle #3: In order to achieve oneness, a couple must share a strong commitment to God's purpose for marriage.

HomeBuilders Principle #4: When we yield to God and build together from His blueprints, we **begin** the process of experiencing oneness.

HomeBuilders Principle #5: The basis for my acceptance of my mate is faith in God's character and trustworthiness.

HomeBuilders Principle #6: A godly marriage is not created by finding a perfect, flawless person, but **is** created by allowing God's perfect love and acceptance to flow through one imperfect person—you—toward another imperfect person—your mate.

HomeBuilders Principle #7: A godly marriage is established and experienced as we leave, cleave, and become one flesh.

HomeBuilders Principle #8: Only Spiritual Christians can have a hope of building godly homes.

HomeBuilders Principle #9: The home built by God requires both the husband and wife to yield to the Holy Spirit in every area of their lives.

HomeBuilders Principle #10: The heritage you were handed is not as important as the legacy you will leave.

HomeBuilders Principle #11: The legacy you leave is determined by the life you live.

HomeBuilders Principle #12: Your marriage should leave a legacy of love that will influence future generations.

Men Only

HomeBuilders Principle for Men #1: A husband who is becoming a servant-leader is one who is in the process of denying himself daily for his wife.

HomeBuilders Principle for Men #2: The husband who is becoming an unselfish lover of his wife is one who is putting his wife's needs above his own.

HomeBuilders Principle for Men #3: The husband who is becoming a caring head of his house is one who encourages his wife to grow and become all that God intended her to be.

Women Only

HomeBuilders Principle for Women #1: Becoming a successful wife requires that a woman make her husband her #2 priority after her relationship with God.

HomeBuilders Principle for Women #2: The wife who is becoming an unselfish lover of her husband is one who is putting her husband's needs above her own.

HomeBuilders Principle for Women #3: In order for a husband to successfully lead, he must have a wife who willingly submits to his leadership.

HomeBuilders Principle for Women #4: A successful wife is one who respects her husband.

Defeating selfishness and isolation is essential in building oneness and a godly marriage.

List below the names of the couples in your group and something unique to help you remember them:

_____   _____

_____   _____

_____   _____

_____   _____

_____   _____

_____   _____

_____   _____

A. A Cause of Failure in Marriage

No one starts out intending to fail in a marriage, but many do. Many homes are being built, but increasingly it seems that few succeed at building a godly marriage.

1. Why do you think couples are so naturally close during dating —and then often so distant after they marry?

_____

_____

2. One of the main reasons people get married is to find intimacy —a close, personal relationship with another person. Yet it does not seem to come naturally. Why do you think this is true?

_____

_____

3. What do you see in Isaiah 53:6a which would explain the failure to achieve intimacy in marriage?

_____

_____

4. It is easier to see selfishness in your mate than in yourself. What are some of the ways you struggle with selfishness in your marriage? List at least three.

_____

_____

_____

B. Results of Going Your Own Way

1. How have the above examples of "going your own way" affected your marriage? Be specific.

_____

_____

_____

2. Selfishness in a relationship leads to isolation. (Instead of the closeness we want, we end up being separated or set apart from each other.)

`i-so-`lā-tion (n) The condition of being alone, separated, solitary, set apart (from the Latin *insulatus*, made into an island). (from *The American Heritage Dictionary*)

Why is isolation in marriage an enemy to be feared?

_____

_____

_____

_____

3. Even stronger than fear of isolation from one's mate is the fear of being rejected by him or her. Why do you think this is so? Why are people willing to tolerate isolation, rather than working to build oneness and harmony in marriage?

_____

_____

_____

_____

_____

■

The above issues lead us to consider these questions:

■ How can a couple defeat selfishness and thus avoid being isolated from one another?

■ How can a couple build a home that will withstand the pressures that are destroying marriages today?

The answer is found in a story Jesus told about two attempts to build a home. . . .

■

(to be completed as a couple)

With your mate, read Jesus' story in Matthew 7:24–27 and complete the following chart:

What were the two foundations?
How were the two men described?
Both men heard Christ's words; what was each man's response?
What was the ultimate result?

As a couple, decide which of these statements comes closest to matching your response to this story:

☐ It's a nice story, but we don't see how it fits our marriage.
☐ We get the point about putting good advice into practice, but we're not convinced Christ's advice is best.
☐ We think a lot of what Jesus said is helpful and we'll consider it.
☐ We're willing to follow Christ's teachings in our marriage.
☐ We enthusiastically embrace Christ's teachings in our marriage.

Summarize the point this story makes for your life and marriage:

_____

_____

C. The Hope for Defeating Selfishness and Isolation

> **HomeBuilders Principle #1:** It is only as you yield and submit your life to God, obey His Word, and deny yourself that you can experience intimacy and build a godly marriage.

1. If success in life—and marriage—rests on doing what Christ said, read the following scriptures and discover what He said about defeating selfishness:

John 12:24, 25 _____

_____

Luke 14:27–30 _____

_____

Mark 10:43–45 _____

_____

2. How do these three statements by Christ apply to defeating selfishness and isolation in marriage? In **your** marriage?

_____

_____

3. To pay the price, to die to self, and to serve your mate—these are hard things to do. Read John 6:60, 61, 66–69 to find two different responses to Jesus' teachings. Summarize the two responses in the boxes below:

1.	2.

Which response is closest to your reaction to Jesus' instructions about defeating selfishness?

_____

_____

4. What point from this session do you need to "obey" in your marriage? What do you need to do?

_____

_____

5. Living in victory over selfishness is a lifelong process. A husband or wife needs the guidance of God's Word. In the passage below, underline the three building blocks which produce solid benefits in a home.

> By wisdom a house is built,
> and by understanding it is established;
> and by knowledge the rooms are filled
> with all precious and pleasant riches.
> Proverbs 24:3, 4

Scripture provides the raw materials, the building blocks that we need to build a marriage marked by oneness and harmony instead of isolation. The next six sessions of this first study will explore the blueprints found in God's Word for building your home. Your discovery and application of these truths will result in a home that is built and filled ("established") with **all** precious and pleasant riches!

Make a date with your mate to meet in the next few days to complete **HomeBuilders Project #1.** This will aid you as a couple in continuing the process of building your marriage. Your leader will ask you at the next session to share one thing from this experience.

Date	Time	Location

■

■ **Staying Close**   by Dennis Rainey

This book by the director of FamilyLife expands on the subjects covered in this study and in our FamilyLife Marriage Conference. Chapters 1-3 will help you consider further the issues discussed in this session.

As a Couple—5–10 Minutes

Complete any activity from the first session that you may not have had time to complete or want to study further. Share what was most meaningful to you in Session One.

Individually—15–20 Minutes

Write your answers to these questions:

1. Recall some moments during the past year when you felt close to your mate.

_____

_____

2. During those times, how was selfishness defeated?

_____

_____

3. Read John 12:24, 25; Luke 14:27–30; and Mark 10:43–45. Finish this sentence: "When I'm being selfish, I need to . . . "

_____

_____

4. Read 1 Peter 3:8–12. List things you should do when your mate is being selfish:

_____

_____

_____

5. What one thing will you do this week to show an unselfish attitude toward your mate and obey the words of Christ?

_____

_____

Interact As a Couple—25–30 Minutes

1. Share your answers to the above questions and the discoveries that you made in answering them.

2. Discuss and answer the following:

No one "enjoys" being told that he or she is being selfish. Your marriage can benefit by knowing how to approach one another when the other mate is being selfish. Wisdom, gentleness, and a proper approach can all help bring the selfish one back to a correct perspective. Share a couple of ways your mate could **help you** deal with your selfishness:

_____

_____

(It would be a good idea to get your mate's "permission" before applying these suggestions.)

3. Agree on any action you will take.

4. Close your time together by praying for one another.

Remember to bring your calendar for **Make a Date** to the next session.

Oneness in marriage is achieved as both husband and wife yield to God and work together in building their home from the same set of blueprints: the Bible.

1. What was the most meaningful result of the last session as you worked with your mate to overcome selfishness and isolation? What have you discovered about yourself and your mate?

_____

_____

_____

In the first session, you saw that selfishness produces isolation in marriage. Neither is a part of God's plan for marriage—instead, He wants to defeat them. Let's look at His blueprint for replacing isolation (a natural result) with oneness (a supernatural result).

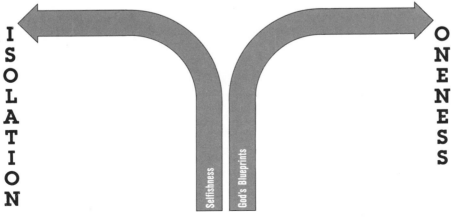

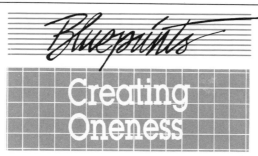

A. The Benefits of Oneness

1. What do the following scriptures teach us abut some of the benefits of oneness in a relationship?

Psalm 133:1 _____

_____

Ecclesiastes 4:9–12 _____

_____

2. From your experience, what are some other benefits you gain from being one with your mate?

_____

_____

> **HomeBuilders Principle #2: Oneness in marriage involves complete unity with each other.**

B. Achieving Oneness

1. What would society say is the way to achieve oneness in marriage?

_____

_____

2. What important factors are missing from most secular instructions in achieving oneness?

_____

_____

3. In his letter to the church at Philippi, Paul addressed the issue of oneness among Christians. The points he made also show us how to achieve oneness within marriage:

1 "If therefore there is any encouragement in Christ,
   if there is any consolation of love,
     if there is any fellowship of the Spirit,
      if any affection and compassion,

2 make my joy complete by
   being of the same mind,
     maintaining the same love,
      united in spirit,
       intent on one purpose.

3 Do nothing from selfishness or empty conceit,
   but with humility of mind
     let each of you regard one another
     as more important than himself;

4 do not merely look out for your own personal interests,
   but also for the interests of others."

Philippians 2:1–4

30

What does Paul say in verses 3 and 4 that relates to what you learned from Session One about selfishness?

_____

_____

4. Share an illustration of a time when you did or did not deny yourself for your mate:

_____

_____

What was the result? _____

_____

5. What does verse 2 say to you about how to achieve oneness in a relationship?

_____

_____

HomeBuilders Principle #3: In order to achieve oneness, a couple must share a strong commitment to God's purpose for marriage.

C. God's Purpose for Marriage

1. Match the following scriptures with God's five purposes for marriage:

a. Genesis 1:26, 27	MANAGE God's Creation
b. Genesis 1:28a	MODEL Christ's Relationship to His Church
c. Genesis 1:28b	MIRROR God's Image
d. Genesis 2:18 & 1 Corinthians 11:11	MULTIPLY a Godly Heritage
e. Ephesians 5:31	MUTUALLY Complete One Another

2. Why is each purpose important in a marriage? List ways each can be applied in your marriage today.

_____

_____

_____

> **HomeBuilders Principle #4: When we yield to God and build together from His blueprints, we *begin* the process of experiencing oneness.**

Construction
(to be completed as a couple)

Let's consider one of the five purposes for marriage:

1. How well is your marriage mirroring God's image—representing Him—in the areas and relationships listed below? **Rate yourselves on a scale of 1 (lowest) to 10 (highest) in how your marriage reflects God to these people:**

We mirror God's	to each other	to our children	to our neighbors	to co-workers
• . . . perfect love for imperfect people;				
• . . . loving-kindness, by serving to meet needs;				
• . . . commit-ment, by patient support;				
• . . . peace, by resolving conflicts.				

2. Are there any hindrances to your mirroring God's image in your marriage? Discuss with each other what needs to be done to remove any barriers.

_____

_____

3. What did you learn about your marriage from this evaluation?

_____

_____

_____

_____

Make a date with your mate to meet in the next few days to complete **HomeBuilders Project #2.** Your leader will ask at the next session for you to share one thing from this experience.

Date	Time	Location

■

■ Staying Close

by Dennis Rainey

"God's Purpose for Oneness" and "The Master Plan for Oneness" are the subjects covered in Chapters 11–12.

As a Couple—5–10 Minutes

Review Session Two and complete any previous sessions and/or projects that are not finished. Discuss those points that stand out in your mind.

Individually—15–20 Minutes

Answer each of the following questions and prepare to discuss them with your mate.

1. What would our closest friends say is the purpose of our marriage?

_____

_____

2. In which of God's purposes are we succeeding? (manage, model, mirror, multiply, mutually complete)

_____

_____

3. Which ones need work in our marriage? In what way?

_____

_____

4. What hinders our success in accomplishing these purposes?

_____

_____

5. What tough decisions need to be made **now**? In the next six to twelve months?

_____

_____

6. What one step could we take this week to move toward fulfilling one of God's purposes in our marriage?

_____

_____

Interact As a Couple—25–30 Minutes

Discuss with your mate your reflections on and discoveries from the above questions. Please be sure to **agree** on any action step and **how** it will be implemented. Close your time together by praying for one another and for your success in fulfilling God's purposes for your marriage.

Remember to bring your calendar for **Make a Date** to the next session.

Oneness in marriage requires receiving your mate as God's perfect provision for your needs.

1. One thing I **would not** want to change about my mate is . . .

_____

_____

2. What are your mate's three greatest strengths—and how do they complement your own strengths and weaknesses? *

_____

_____

_____

_____

_____

_____

_____

_____

* Questions taken from **The Questions Book for Marriage Intimacy** by Dennis and Barbara Rainey. Published by FamilyLife, 1988.

3. Share your answer to one of these questions from **HomeBuilders Project #2**:

■ What would your closest friends say is the purpose of your marriage?

_____

_____

■ What one step did you take since our last session toward fulfilling one of God's purposes in your marriage?

_____

_____

_____

We have seen that selfishness produces isolation in marriage, while following God's blueprints leads to oneness. Now we will explore the importance of receiving one's mate as God's special gift for our aloneness needs.

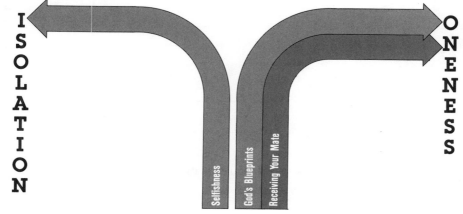

In Genesis 2:18–23, we find the familiar story of Adam and Eve. Our familiarity with Scriptures such as this can blind us to profound insights—insights that, when applied, can strengthen every marriage. Let's look at what we can learn from this passage to help us achieve oneness in marriage:

A. Everyone's Need (Genesis 2:18)

1. What need did God build into Adam that was not filled by God's personal presence? What was "not good" about Adam as God created him?

_____

_____

2. What are some likely reasons why God made Adam incomplete?

_____

_____

3. Identify two or three ways you are incomplete and need your mate:

_____

_____

_____

B. Awareness of Need (Genesis 2:19, 20)

1. What did naming animals have to do with Adam's aloneness? How aware of being alone do you think Adam was before he named the animals?

_____

_____

2. Why did God want Adam to see his need for a mate?

_____

_____

3. What are some ways you see your need for your mate today that you did not recognize when you first got married?

_____

_____

4. How do you think your awareness of needing your mate may change in the next five years?

_____

_____

5. At the beginning of your relationship with your mate, how aware was God of all your needs (past, present, future)?

_____

_____

_____

C. God's Provision for Our Need (Genesis 2:21, 22)

1. List five things God did in these verses:

a. _____   b. _____

c. _____   d. _____

e. _____

2. Which of these actions seems most significant to you? Why?

_____

_____

D. Our Response to God's Provision (Genesis 2:23)

1. What had Eve done up to this point to warrant Adam's acceptance?

_____

_____

2. Why was Adam able to immediately recognize Eve as the mate who would fulfill his need?

_____

_____

3. Who did Adam know better, Eve or God? _____

4. Are you more a student of:

☐ your mate (strengths, weaknesses, etc.)
OR
☐ the One who provided him/her for you?

> **HomeBuilders Principle #5: The basis for my acceptance of my mate is faith in God's character and trustworthiness.**

5. What causes us to reject rather than receive our mate?

_____

_____

6. Since God provided your mate, can you reject your mate without rejecting God? Why?

_____

_____

7. Consider the results of not receiving your mate. Describe such a marriage ten to twenty years from now.

_____

_____

_____

_____

8. Which of these statements could you most readily apply in your marriage: "Weaknesses in my mate are . . ."

☐ a. opportunities for me to be needed.

☐ b. tools of God to cause me to trust Him.

☐ c. only changed through a climate of loving acceptance.

HomeBuilders Principle #6: A godly marriage *is not* created by finding a perfect, flawless person, but *is* created by allowing God's perfect love and acceptance to flow through one imperfect person—you—toward another imperfect person—your mate.

Construction
(to be completed as a couple)

1. Individually, list ways **you see** your mate needing you. (Try to list ten if time permits.)

_____

_____

_____

_____

_____

_____

2. Share your list with your mate.

Make a date with your mate to meet in the next few days to complete **HomeBuilders Project #3.** This time for the two of you is as important as the time for the sessions. Your leader will ask at the next session for you to share one thing from this experience.

Date	Time	Location

■

■ **Building Your Mate's Self-Esteem**   by Dennis and Barbara Rainey

Accepting your mate is one of the cornerstones of a godly marriage.
Dennis and Barbara's book, **Building Your Mate's Self-Esteem**, can
help you express your acceptance and belief in each other. An
intensely practical book, it will teach you how to deal with the
haunting problems of the past, how to give your mate the freedom to
fail, and how to help your mate be liberated from questions of
self-doubt.

■ **Staying Close**   by Dennis Rainey

"Why It's So Hard to Keep All Those Plates Spinning," "I Expected Him
to Meet Me Halfway But..." and "You Can't Expect to Be Selfish in a
Three-legged Race" are the subjects covered in Chapters 5-7. These
will help you consider further the issues discussed in this session.
Before your next session you will want to read Chapter 8-10, which
deal with three additional threats to oneness and intimacy.

■

There are two **HomeBuilders Projects** for you to choose from for this session. Project #3A is for those who have not attended a FamilyLife Marriage Conference. Project #3B is for Conference alumni.

Individually—40 Minutes

A. Write out the answers to the following questions in the form of a love letter. Use page 52 for your letter (30 minutes).

1. What were the qualities that attracted me the most to you when we first met?

2. Do I see and accept you as you really are? What have I not accepted in you?

3. Do you see and accept me as I really am? In what areas do I feel that you have not accepted me? How does this make me feel?

B. Spend time in prayer, individually (10 minutes).

1. Confess to God any rejection of, withdrawal from or bitterness toward your mate as sin. Thank God for His forgiveness and the cleansing blood of Christ.

"If we confess our sins, He is faithful and righteous to forgive us our sins and to cleanse us from all unrighteousness" (1 John 1:9).

2. Commit to God totally, by faith, to receive your mate based upon the integrity and sovereignty of God. Be sure to put this commitment in your love letter.

3. Commit to God to trust Him with your mate's weaknesses and to love your mate unconditionally with Christ's love (apart from performance). Be certain you put this commitment in your love letter.

Interact As a Couple—15–20 Minutes.

1. Share and discuss your letter.

2. Verbalize to your mate the commitment you made to God during your individual prayer time.

3. Close your time together by taking turns thanking God for each other.

Remember to bring your calendar for **Make a Date** to the next session.

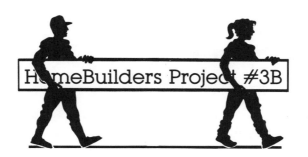

As a Couple—5-10 Minutes

Review the concept we studied in Session Three. Share what really impressed you in the study. Go back over any sections you wanted to discuss with your mate but were unable to.

Individually—25-30 Minutes

Complete the project below. (You may need more time—that's fine. It is important to take enough time to accurately express to your mate how you feel about him/her.)

1. Do an inventory of the ways your mate is meeting your needs. Try to list 25 or more if you can. (List on a separate sheet of paper.)

2. Identify which of those are the five most important ways you need him or her.

3. Identify those differences in your mate that God uses to complete you.

_____

_____

_____

4. Identify one or two areas in which you may have been rejecting or not totally accepting your mate. What has been the result of that rejection for you? For your mate?

_____

_____

_____

_____

5. Do you need to ask forgiveness for your lack of acceptance toward your mate? If appropriate, express this to your mate.

Interact As a Couple—15–20 Minutes

1. Share the results of your project with your mate.

2. Affirm (or reaffirm) to your mate your acceptance of him or her as God's perfect provision for your needs.

3. Close your time together in prayer, thanking God for one another.

Remember to bring your calendar for **Make a Date** to the next session.

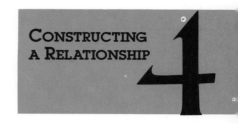

Focus

The process of becoming one requires that a couple construct their marriage by leaving parents, cleaving to each other, and becoming one flesh.

1. What was one of the first difficult challenges in your commitment to each other that you faced in the early years of your marriage?

_____

_____

2. How did that challenge affect your commitment to each other?

_____

In Session Three we saw that with our confidence in God's character and trustworthiness, we can totally accept and receive our mate as His provision for our needs. Many couples today have yet to realize that they have not been following the biblical blueprints for becoming one. God's blueprints for the lifelong process of constructing a godly marriage have three practical phases.

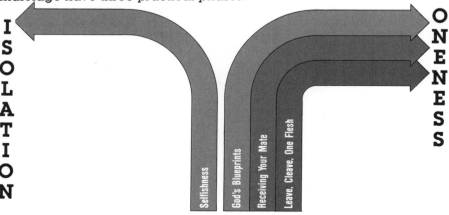

ISOLATION

ONENESS

Selfishness

God's Blueprints

Receiving Your Mate

Leave, Cleave, One Flesh

A. Phase 1—Leave (Genesis 2:24)

1. Once a couple has received each other as God's gift (Genesis 2:18–23), they must leave their parents. What factors are involved in "leaving" one's parents? How do people establish and maintain independence from parents?

_____

_____

_____

2. Answer the question that fits your situation. What are some ways:

a. couples in the first few years of marriage do not leave their parents?

b. couples in later years of marriage do not leave their parents?

c. couples who marry later in life and do not leave parents and/or leave their independent lifestyle?

_____

_____

3. What can happen in a marriage when:

a. parents are "too clingy"?

_____

_____

b. the son/daughter is dependent on parents and not on his or her mate?

_____

_____

4. Ephesians 6:2, 3 commands us, "Honor your father and mother." What are some practical ways of honoring your parents and providing for them without becoming dependent on them?

_____

_____

5. Are there ways you and your mate have not left your parents? How?

_____

_____

6. What practical advice would you give to:

a. the dependent son/daughter? _____

_____

b. the son/daughter whose parents are "too clingy"? _____

_____

B. Phase 2—Cleave (Genesis 2:24b)

1. The second step in constructing a solid marriage is to "cleave" to your mate. What does the phrase "cleave to his wife" mean in this verse?

_____

_____

2. What is the relationship between leaving your parents and cleaving to your mate?

_____

_____

3. What factors in society and in marriage make cleaving difficult?

_____

_____

4. Malachi 2:15b, 16, says, "'Take heed, then, to your spirit, and let no one deal treacherously against the wife of your youth. For I hate divorce,' says the Lord . . ." Why is cleaving so important to God?

_____

_____

5. What are some reasons why commitment is important to a marriage relationship? Why is your mate's commitment important to you?

_____

_____

_____

C. Phase 3—Become One Flesh (Genesis 2:24c)

1. The third step in the construction process is to "become one flesh"—to establish physical intimacy. What insights does Matthew 19:6 add to your understanding of becoming one flesh?

_____

_____

2. How is becoming one flesh something that happens at a point in time as well as an ongoing process?

_____

_____

3. Why is becoming one flesh important in achieving oneness in marriage?

_____

_____

4. List the three most romantic times you and your mate have experienced:

_____

_____

_____

Share the list with your mate. Then together, look for a common thread in these incidents which drew you together and which you can share with the group.

_____

_____

> **HomeBuilders Principle #7: A godly marriage is established and experienced as we leave, cleave, and become one flesh.**

D. The Result—Naked and Unashamed (Genesis 2:25)

1. The result of Adam and Eve fulfilling the three phases of construction was that they were "naked and unashamed." What is the significance of a couple's being "naked and unashamed"? How is this a picture of oneness?

_____

_____

_____

$2.$ Why is your acceptance of and commitment to your mate important in achieving openness and transparency in your relationship? What additional light does 1 John 4:18 shed on this process?

> There is no fear in love;
> but perfect love casts out fear.
>   1 John 4:18

_____

_____

_____

_____

_____

_____

■

Construction

(to be completed as a couple)

Meet with your mate and choose one of these three projects:

A. Phase 1—Leave (Work Together.)

1. In what ways have either you or your mate not left your parents?

_____

2. What action(s) do you need to take—while still honoring your parents?

_____

B. Phase 2—Cleave (Answer Individually, Then Share.)

1. What three things communicate cleaving/commitment:

to you? _____

to your mate? _____

2. What are some areas in which you are not cleaving?

_____

C. Phase 3—Become One Flesh (Write Answers Individually and Discuss on the Way Home.)

1. How can I improve our sex life?

_____

_____

2. What do you wish I would or wouldn't do in making love?

_____

_____

3. What do you enjoy most about our sex life? *

_____

_____

LIST ONE ACTION you will take this week to apply what you have learned:

_____

_____

* The last three questions are from **The Questions Book for Marriage Intimacy** by Dennis and Barbara Rainey. Published by FamilyLife, 1988.

Make a date with your mate to meet in the next few days to complete **HomeBuilders Project #4.** Your leader will ask at the next session for you to share one thing from this experience.

_____   _____   _____

Date   Time   Location

■

■ **The Questions Book for Marriage Intimacy**   by Dennis and
Barbara Rainey

The Questions Book for Marriage Intimacy gives you 31 questions
you've never thought to ask your mate. Questions that will ignite your
curiosity and rekindle your fascination for each other. A great
marriage takes communication, and **The Questions Book for
Marriage Intimacy** will guide and encourage you and your mate to
practice heart-to-heart communication. These questions will spark
many memorable hours of sharing, sharpen your understanding of
your mate, and stimulate closeness in new areas of your marriage.

■ **Staying Close**   by Dennis Rainey

"Communication or Isolation?" "To Turn Conflict into Oneness, Begin
to Listen!" "The Secret of Loving Confrontation," "Returning a Blessing
for an Insult," and "What Makes a Great Lover?" are the subjects
covered in Chapters 18–22.

■

As a Couple—5–10 Minutes

Review the three phases of constructing a great marriage: leave, cleave, and become one flesh. Then select one of the following projects that is most relevant to your marriage today.

Individually—25–30 Minutes

PHASE 1 PROJECT—**LEAVING PARENTS**
PHASE 2 PROJECT—**CLEAVING**
PHASE 3 PROJECT—**BECOMING ONE FLESH**

■

PHASE 1 PROJECT
LEAVING PARENTS

1. Use the chart on the next page to rank yourself and your mate in each area of leaving your parents:

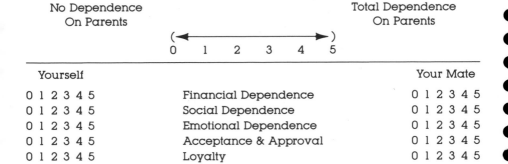

	No Dependence On Parents						Total Dependence On Parents
	(←					→)	
	0	1	2	3	4	5	

Yourself		Your Mate
0 1 2 3 4 5	Financial Dependence	0 1 2 3 4 5
0 1 2 3 4 5	Social Dependence	0 1 2 3 4 5
0 1 2 3 4 5	Emotional Dependence	0 1 2 3 4 5
0 1 2 3 4 5	Acceptance & Approval	0 1 2 3 4 5
0 1 2 3 4 5	Loyalty	0 1 2 3 4 5

2. List any actions you may need to take.

_____

_____

3. List any suggestions you have for your mate and note how you can help him/her avoid dependence on parents.

_____

_____

Now turn to page 72 and complete the section entitled "Interact As A Couple."

■

PHASE 2 PROJECT
CLEAVING

1. Answer the following Yes/No, True/False questions.

Y N   Do you ever threaten to leave your mate?

T F   My mate is secure in my commitment to him/her.

T F   I am more committed to my mate than to my career.

T F   My mate knows I am more committed to him/her than to my career.

T F   I am more committed to my mate than to my children.

T F   My mate knows I am more committed to him/her than to my children.

T F   I am more committed to my mate than to my activities.

Y N   Do you emotionally leave your mate by withdrawing for an extended period of time because of conflict?

Y N   Do you mentally leave your mate by staying preoccupied with other things?

Y N   Are you passive about helping your mate solve his/her problems?

Y N   Are you interested in your mate's needs and actively doing what you can to meet them?

2. Now go back through the above list and determine in what areas you need to demonstrate a stronger commitment to your mate.

Area	**COMMITMENT TO CLEAVE** Action Point

3. Do you need to ask your mate's forgiveness in an area? If so, in which one(s)?

_____

_____

_____

4. Write out your plan for communicating your commitment to your mate. Be specific.

_____

_____

Now turn to page 72 and complete the section entitled "Interact As A Couple."

■

PHASE 3 PROJECT
BECOMING ONE FLESH

Becoming one flesh **at a point in time**

1. How has leaving and cleaving made becoming one flesh easier? What changes do you need to make in these areas?

_____

_____

2. What circumstances or settings seem best for you to share intimately with one another? List a few.

_____

_____

3. What attitudes need to be present in you and your mate as you come together?

_____

_____

4. Write your mate a note: "It pleases me most when you . . . "

_____

_____

Becoming one flesh **over a lifetime**

1. How are you more one flesh now than when you first married?

_____

_____

2. In what one or two areas of your marriage do you need to continue to work at being one with one another?

_____

_____

3. Looking into the future, write a letter to your mate of what you expect your relationship to be like when you are both in your 70s or 80s. Include in this how you will feel about him/her, how you will have shared both good and bad, and how you will have weathered storms together. Talk about how you envision your last ten to fifteen years together. Read your letter to him or her.

Now complete the section below.

Interact As a Couple—15–20 Minutes

1. Share what both of you wrote in completing your project. Look each other in the eyes as you discuss your writings.

2. Work together to identify one or two actions for you to take in the coming week in response to your discussion.

3. Make a date as soon as possible to have a two- or three-hour block of time to be alone together for more communication.

Remember to bring your calendar for **Make a Date** to the next session.

Focus

There are three biblical responsibilities
God wants a husband to assume
toward his wife:
servant-leadership, unselfish loving,
and caring.

1. What various roles must you fill to be a success as a man in our society today?

_____

_____

_____

2. What kinds of preparation (schooling, training courses, books, etc.) did you have for filling these roles?

_____

_____

_____

3. What factors in society and within marriage make it difficult today to be an effective husband? What is your greatest struggle in being a good husband?

_____

_____

_____

_____

Oneness results when a couple follows God's blueprints, receives one another as God's gift, and then constructs their marriage by leaving parents, cleaving to each other, and becoming one flesh. In this session, we will discover what character traits are essential if we are to be the husbands God created us to be.

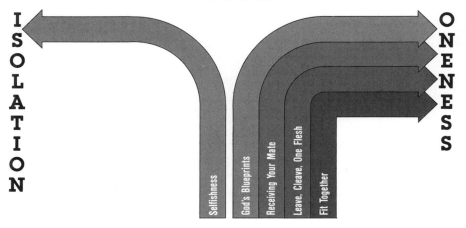

It is vital that you understand from Scripture your responsibility as a husband. Only as you and your wife understand the unique roles which God has given to you can the oneness God intended in marriage be obtained.

Because there is a great deal of confusion about the roles of men and women today, this session will be spent helping you write a biblical job description for being a husband—the head of your home.

A. The First Responsibility—BECOMING A SERVANT-LEADER

1. How is a husband's position as leader illustrated in Ephesians 5:23?

_____

_____

2. What are the responsibilities involved in being "the head" of your wife, a group of people, or an organization?

_____

_____

_____

3. What additional insights do you gain about leadership from Mark 10:42–45? What is servant-leadership?

_____

_____

_____

4. Which of those concepts is the most profound to you as you think of your leadership in your home? Why?

_____

_____

_____

5. How would becoming a servant-leader change a man who:

a. tends to be **passive** and does not accept his responsibilities?

_____

_____

b. is **dictatorial** and refuses to listen to his wife?

_____

_____

6. How would becoming a servant-leader affect the ability of your wife to be submissive? How would she respond in other areas if you were more of a servant-leader?

_____

_____

_____

_____

HomeBuilders Principle for Men #1: A husband who is becoming a servant-leader is one who is in the process of denying himself daily for his wife.

Responsibility One:
BECOMING A SERVANT-LEADER

List one to three practical ways in which you can demonstrate servant-leadership to your wife in the coming weeks:

_____

_____

_____

_____

_____

_____

B. The Second Responsibility—UNSELFISH LOVING

1. According to Ephesians 5:25–27, why is the second responsibility of a husband so important?

_____

_____

2. Verse 25 says Christ "gave Himself up for her." How does this kind of love, this denial of self, communicate love to your wife? Why is this so important?

_____

_____

3. How does God describe love in these other passages?

Philippians 2:3 _____

_____

1 Corinthians 13:4–7 _____

_____

John 15:13 _____

_____

4. Which of the preceding descriptions of love is the most profound to you? Why?

_____

_____

5. Which of those descriptions of love does your wife need most? How can you demonstrate that love to her?

_____

_____

HomeBuilders Principle for Men #2: The husband who is becoming an unselfish lover of his wife is one who is putting his wife's needs above his own.

Responsibility Two:
UNSELFISH LOVING

1. List five things you enjoy that could, if denied, demonstrate unselfish love to your wife:

_____

_____

_____

_____

_____

2. What would you have to do in this self-denial to make it a willing act of love and not a grudging duty?

_____

_____

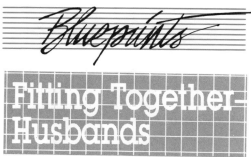

C. The Third Responsibility—CARING

1. What does Ephesians 5:28–30 add to your view of your responsibility to your wife? Why is this truth important?

_____

_____

2. "Nourish" means to foster growth. What elements of nourishment does your wife need from you to help her grow?

_____

_____

3. The term "cherish" is from the Greek word meaning "to incubate or brood," and indicates esteeming someone as a priority. How can you show your wife you esteem and value her? Be specific.

_____

_____

HomeBuilders Principle for Men #3: The husband who is becoming a caring head of his house is one who encourages his wife to grow and become all that God intended her to be.

Responsibility Three:
CARING

1. One aspect of leadership is bringing appropriate resources to a situation to help others become successful. What resources do you need to use in order to nourish and cherish your wife so that she can succeed as a woman, wife, and mother (help with her schedule, assist with a problem, give or get direct help with a task, provide encouragement, spend time with her, etc.)?

_____

_____

_____

2. Review the three **Construction** projects you have done in this session and choose one act of servant-leadership, unselfish loving, or caring for your wife which you will share with the group and for which you will agree to be accountable to the group by the next session.

_____

_____

Make a date with your mate to meet in the next few days to complete **HomeBuilders Project #5**.

_____ _____ _____
Date   Time   Location

■

■ **Rocking the Roles**　　　by Robert Lewis and William Hendricks

This book provides a balanced, biblical guide to understanding marital roles.

■ **Building Your Mate's Self-Esteem**　　by Dennis and Barbara Rainey

In **Building Your Mate's Self-Esteem**, you will find clues to understanding your wife's self-esteem, laws that will help you to free your mate from her past, and building blocks to strengthen her self-esteem.

■ **The Questions Book for Marriage Intimacy**　　by Dennis and Barbara Rainey

The Questions Book for Marriage Intimacy gives you 31 questions you've never thought to ask your mate. Questions that will ignite your curiosity and rekindle your fascination for each other. A great marriage takes communication and **The Questions Book for Marriage Intimacy** will guide and encourage you and your mate to practice heart-to-heart communication. These questions will spark many memorable hours of sharing, sharpen your understanding of your mate, and stimulate closeness in new areas of your marriage.

■ **Staying Close**　　　　　　by Dennis Rainey

"The Making of a Servant-leader" is the subject covered in Chapter 14.

■

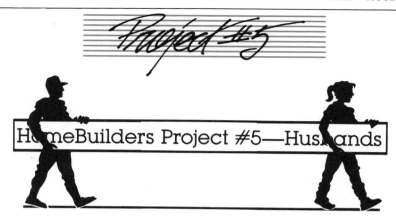

HomeBuilders Project #5—Husbands

Set aside an hour and a half to complete this project.

1. Review the lesson on the responsibilities of a husband. (Complete any undone **Construction** projects.)

2. Ask God to show you how you are to be the best possible husband for your wife.

3. Make a list of ten to fifteen of your wife's needs, grouping them in the following areas of life (you may wish to schedule a special time to ask her what they really are):

Physical	Social	Spiritual	Mental	Emotional
_____	_____	_____	_____	_____
_____	_____	_____	_____	_____
_____	_____	_____	_____	_____

4. List three of the above needs which seem to be of greatest importance to her at this time.

_____   _____   _____

5. After verifying these needs with your wife, list appropriate actions you need to take to help meet those needs, demonstrating your desire to be God's man in her life.

_____

_____

_____

_____

_____

6. Pray again, asking God to give you wisdom and skill in meeting your wife's needs effectively.

7. Write your wife's needs on a 3 x 5 card and place it where you will see it daily (mirror, desk drawer, etc.) as a reminder of how you can meet her needs in a practical way.

8. Be prepared to share next time your successes and/or failures. Your responses will encourage others in the group.

Remember to bring your calendar for **Make a Date** to the next session.

There are four biblical responsibilities God wants a wife to assume toward her husband: making marriage a priority, unselfish love, submission, and respect.

1. List some words that describe each point of view:

	SOCIETY'S VIEW	GOD'S VIEW
Woman		
Wife		
Mother		

2. Women are being told today that they need to be successful. What do you think makes a successful wife?

_____

_____

_____

3. What are some of your struggles in trying to succeed as a wife?

_____

_____

_____

Oneness results when a couple follows God's blueprints, receives one another as God's gift, and then constructs their marriage by leaving parents, cleaving to each other, and becoming one flesh.

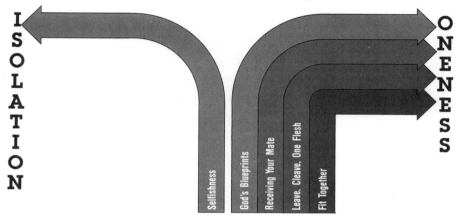

It is vital that you understand from Scripture your responsibility as a wife. Only as you and your husband understand the unique roles which God has given to you can the oneness God intended in marriage be obtained.

A. The First Responsibility—MAKING YOUR MARRIAGE A PRIORITY

1. What does it mean for a wife "to look well to the ways of her household"? (Proverbs 31:27)

_____

_____

2. What happens to your relationship with your husband when you do or do not "look well" to your marriage?

WHEN I DO "LOOK WELL"	WHEN I DO NOT "LOOK WELL"

3. In the "IDEAL WIFE" column below, rank these items by numbering them from 1–13 to show the priorities that make a successful wife. Then, in the "ME" column, show where your priorities currently are.

IDEAL WIFE	ME		IDEAL WIFE	ME		IDEAL WIFE	ME	
☐	☐	Children	☐	☐	House/Yard	☐	☐	Husband
☐	☐	Education	☐	☐	Job/Career	☐	☐	Friends
☐	☐	Relatives	☐	☐	Community Service	☐	☐	Church
☐	☐	Social Activities	☐	☐	Appearance	☐	☐	TV
			☐	☐	Relationship with God			

4. How is the priority you place on your marriage reflected in your schedule?

_____

_____

_____

5. What advice would you give to:

a. the woman who is struggling with her priorities and works outside the home?

_____

_____

_____

b. the woman who, though not struggling, has her priorities out of line?

_____

_____

HomeBuilders Principle for Women #1: Becoming a successful wife requires that a woman make her husband her #2 priority after her relationship with God.

Responsibility One:
MAKING YOUR MARRIAGE A PRIORITY

1. In what ways have you made your relationship with your husband a priority?

_____

_____

2. In what ways does your husband respond when he sees you making your marriage a priority?

_____

_____

3. What are the biggest obstacles you face in making your marriage a priority?

_____

_____

4. What are three things that you can do to make your relationship with your husband your priority in the coming week? Be specific, practical, and make it personal.

_____

_____

_____

Blueprints

Fitting Together—Wives

B. The Second Responsibility—UNSELFISH LOVE

1. The Apostle Paul wrote that older women should "encourage the younger women to love their husbands, . . . " (Titus 2:4). Why do you think this instruction is significant?

_____

_____

2. A problem in our society is that "love" is usually equated with a feeling. We need to look at Scripture to find the full definition of what love is. Write down the insights you gain about love from the following scriptures.

1 Corinthians 13:4–7 _____

_____

_____

John 15:13 _____

_____

Philippians 2:3–4 _____

_____

3. Which of these descriptions of love is the most profound to you in thinking about your relationship with your husband? Why?

_____

_____

4. "The heart of her husband trusts in her" (Proverbs 31:11). Every wife wants a husband who is open, who will share his innermost person with her. Few women, however, realize how insecure and fearful their husbands really are. Your love for your husband has a profound impact on his trust of you and his willingness to be vulnerable.

Evaluate your husband's openness and trust toward you. How is your love affecting his willingness and ability to be transparent with you?

_____

_____

_____

_____

HomeBuilders Principle for Women #2: The wife who is becoming an unselfish lover of her husband is one who is putting her husband's needs above her own.

Responsibility Two:
UNSELFISH LOVE

1. In order to unselfishly love your husband and open your relationship, what rights to which you are clinging do you need to let go?

_____

_____

2. What three things communicate love to your husband? (Not what **you** think communicates love, but what **he** thinks.)

_____

_____

_____

3. What practical way can you demonstrate unselfish love to your husband this week?

_____

_____

_____

C. The Third Responsibility—SUBMISSION

1. According to Ephesians 5:22, a wife should demonstrate both an attitude of submission and the actions that result from it. What reactions does the idea of submission generate among women? Why?

_____

_____

_____

2. Why is submission seen as a threat to women?

_____

_____

3. In what areas do you struggle with submission?

_____

_____

_____

4. What does Scripture say is involved in submission?

1 Peter 2:21–23 _____

1 Peter 3:1, 2 _____

1 Peter 3:3, 4 _____

1 Peter 3:5, 6 _____

Titus 2:5 _____

5. Why is submission to your husband important:

a. to his leadership? _____

_____

b. to his love for you? _____

_____

c. to his care for you? _____

_____

d. to his trust of you? _____

_____

6. What advice would you give to help a wife submit to a husband:

a. who is **passive** and doesn't lead? _____

_____

b. who is a **dictator**, doesn't listen, and demands submission?

_____

_____

> **HomeBuilders Principle for Women #3:** In order for a husband to
> successfully lead, he must have a wife who willingly submits to
> his leadership.

Responsibility Three:
SUBMISSION

What are two ways (two areas) that you can demonstrate submission to your husband? (Be sure to select areas that would really encourage him, not just the areas that would be easiest for you.)

_____

_____

_____

_____

_____

_____

D. The Fourth Responsibility—RESPECT

"And let the wife see that she respects and reverences her husband—
that she notices him, regards him, honors him, prefers him, venerates
and esteems him; and that she defers to him, priases him, and loves
and admires him exceedingly" (Ephesians 5:33b, AMPLIFIED).

1. What are three observations from this paragraph of what it
means to respect your husband?

_____

_____

_____

2. Why do men need their wives' respect? Why is respect important
to an insecure man? What are some specific reasons that **your** husband
needs **your** respect?

_____

_____

3. How do you communicate your respect to your husband?

_____

_____

> **HomeBuilders Principle for Women #4: A successful wife is one
> who respects her husband.**

Responsibility Four:
RESPECT

1. Thoughtfully list some additional ways that you can verbally and actively show respect to your husband. (Think back to those times when he has exemplified confidence in his ability as a man.)

VERBALLY	ACTIVELY
1.	1.
2.	2.
3.	3.

2. Review the four **Construction** projects you have done in this session and choose **one** thing for which you will be accountable to the group to do before the next session—to make your marriage a priority, to express unselfish love, to willingly submit, or to show respect to your husband.

_____

_____

_____

Make a date with your mate to meet in the next few days to complete **HomeBuilders Project #5**. Your leader will ask at the next session for you to share one thing from this experience.

Date	Time	Location

■

■ Rocking the Roles   by Robert Lewis and William Hendricks

This book provides a balanced, biblical guide to understanding marital roles.

■ Building Your Mate's Self-Esteem   by Dennis and Barbara Rainey

In **Building Your Mate's Self-Esteem**, you will find clues to understanding your husband's self-esteem, laws that will help you to free your mate from his past, and building blocks to strengthen his self-esteem.

■ The Questions Book for Marriage Intimacy   by Dennis and Barbara Rainey

The Questions Book for Marriage Intimacy gives you 31 questions you've never thought to ask your mate. Questions that will ignite your curiosity and rekindle your fascination for each other. A great marriage takes communication and **The Questions Book for Marriage Intimacy** will guide and encourage you and your mate to practice heart-to-heart communication. These questions will spark many memorable hours of sharing, sharpen your understanding of your mate, and stimulate closeness in new areas of your marriage.

■ Staying Close   by Dennis Rainey

"How to Love Your Husband" is the subject covered in Chapter 15.

■

HomeBuilders Project #5—Wives

Set aside 60–90 minutes to complete the following project:

$1.$ Review the lesson on the responsibilities of a wife. (Complete any undone **Construction** projects.)

$2.$ Ask God to show you how you are to be the best possible wife for your husband.

$3.$ Make a list of ten to fifteen of your husband's needs, grouping them in the following areas of life (you may schedule a special time to ask him what they really are):

Physical	Social	Spiritual	Mental	Emotional

4. List three of these needs which seem to be of greatest importance to him at this time.

_____   _____   _____

5. After verifying the above needs with your husband, list appropriate actions you need to take to help meet those needs, demonstrating your desire to be God's woman in his life.

_____

_____

_____

6. Pray again, asking God to give you wisdom and skill in meeting your husband's needs effectively.

7. Write your intended actions on a 3 × 5 card and place it where you will see it daily (mirror, purse, etc.) as a reminder of how you can meet his needs in practical ways.

8. Be prepared to share in the next session your successes as well as any possible failures, so that you might encourage others in the group.

Remember to bring your calendar for **Make a Date** to the next session.

The HomeBuilders

C O U P L E S   S E R I E S

"Unless the Lord builds the house,
they labor in vain who build it."
Psalm 127:1

A husband and wife can experience
true oneness only as they live by faith,
in the power of the Holy Spirit.

1. Think back to the childhood tale of "The Three Little Pigs." What is the moral of the story?

_____

_____

2. Compare the lesson of "The Three Little Pigs" with the key point in Jesus' story of the wise and foolish builders (Matthew 7:24–27). What is similar in the two stories? What is the key difference in the conclusion of each story?

_____

_____

3. What is the application for your marriage?

_____

_____

We have spent five sessions exploring God's blueprints for marriage —and putting them to work. In this session we will discover how God equips and empowers us to succeed in our desire to achieve oneness with our mate and with Him.

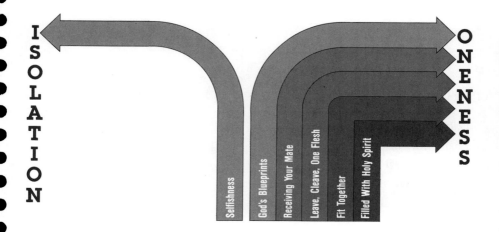

A. The House the Flesh Builds

1. How well do you identify with Paul's lament (Romans 7:18, 19) of his inability to put into practice the truth he believed?

☐ I don't have that trouble at all.

☐ I fall short occasionally.

☐ He said what I feel!

☐ I'm even worse off than he was!

☐ _____

2. Scripture frequently shows that even our best human efforts will not only fall short of success, but will actually end in destruction! What are some of the final results of your own desires and efforts ("the deeds of the flesh") as described in Galatians 5:16–21?

_____

_____

_____

3. How are the "deeds of the flesh" sometimes made evident in your own marriage? (CAUTION: Don't embarrass your mate!)

_____

_____

114

4. 1 Corinthians 2:14–3:3 describes three kinds of people:

The Natural Person (2:14), who has not received Christ as Savior, does not understand spiritual truth, and is in need of spiritual birth.

The Spiritual Person (2:15, 16), who has received Christ and wisely judges or appraises all of life according to God's Word.

The Worldly or Carnal Person (3:1–3), who has received Christ but has not matured as a Christian and who is trying to live the Christian life by human effort.

Which description best fits you? _____

HomeBuilders Principle #8: Only Spiritual Christians can have a hope of building godly homes.

B. The House the Spirit Builds

1. Record below the characteristics listed in Galatians 5:22–26 of a person (or a home) who is yielding to God's Holy Spirit.

_____

_____

_____

2. Pick one part of the fruit of the Spirit that you most need in order to create oneness in your marriage:

_____

How will this quality contribute to oneness in your marriage?

_____

_____

3. Every house has its builder (Hebrews 3:4). Do you feel your home is being built in the energy of the flesh or by the power of the Holy Spirit? Why?

_____

_____

If you are to build a godly home (one that shows forth God's character and attributes: His goodness, faithfulness, justice, love, etc.), you must do so through the power that God supplies. Human ability will never achieve godliness. In the previous session we saw the responsibilities for husbands and wives in Ephesians 5:22–31. This passage is preceded by the command to " . . . be filled with the Holy Spirit" (v. 18).

> **HomeBuilders Principle #9: The home built by God requires both the husband and wife to yield to the Holy Spirit in every area of their lives.**

C. The Holy Spirit in Your Life

1.
In Ephesians 5:18, Paul contrasts being "filled with the Spirit" with being "drunk with wine." What does this comparison say to you about what it means to be filled with the Spirit?

_____

_____

_____

■

To be filled (controlled and empowered) by the Holy Spirit is a process that will be repeated many times as you yield yourself to Christ and His authority over your life. It literally means "keep on being filled."

■

2.
How then can you be filled with the Holy Spirit? The following are some beginning steps. (This process is further developed in the **HomeBuilders Project** to be done after this session.)

a. God will not fill an unclean vessel. What does 1 John 1:9 tell us to do about the sin in our lives? What does it mean to do this?

_____

_____

b. Knowing that we receive Christ by faith, how then do we allow Him to control our lives moment by moment? (Colossians 2:6)

_____

_____

c. What is faith, and why is it important in being filled with the Spirit? (Hebrews 11:1, 6)

_____

_____

d. Does God desire to fill you with His Holy Spirit? (Ephesians 5:18)

_____

e. What has God promised you? (1 John 5:14, 15)

_____

_____

f. Look again at the three circles in part A. Which one represents your life now? Which one do you want to represent your life?

_____

_____

_____

g. After considering these truths, once again distinguish the difference between the wise man and foolish man in Matthew 7. What steps do you need to take to insure that your house is being built upon the Rock?

_____

_____

_____

_____

_____

h. Will you ask God to fill you and control you with His Spirit?

_____

i. Why not take a moment right now and bow in prayer, asking God to empower you with His Spirit?

3. If you confessed your sins, yielded your life to Him, and asked God to fill you with His Spirit, then did He fill you with His Spirit? How can you know?

_____

_____

_____

Construction

(to be completed as a couple)

1. What is the admonition of Galatians 6:7–9, and how can we apply it in building our home?

_____

_____

2. Practically speaking, my greatest hindrance to walking in the power of the Holy Spirit is . . .

_____

_____

3. How can we help and encourage each other to walk in the power of the Holy Spirit?

_____

_____

4. In what practical, everyday situations would the power of the Holy Spirit make a difference in our marriage? (i.e., communication, sex, inlaws, roles, conflict resolution, acceptance, etc.) What one thing can we do to see this difference realized?

_____

_____

_____

Make a Date

Make a date with your mate to meet in the next few days to complete **HomeBuilders Project #6.** This will aid you as a couple in continuing the process of building your marriage. Your leader will ask at the next session for you to share one thing from this experience.

| _____ | _____ | _____ |
| Date | Time | Location |

■

Recommended Reading

■ **The Holy Spirit**   by Dr. Bill Bright

The door to life's greatest adventure—the walk of faith, purpose, and power—can be unlocked through the strength and guidance of the Holy Spirit. Find out who He is, His purpose, and His relationship to you. Basic principles for spiritual growth and ministry effectiveness.

■**Staying Close**   by Dennis Rainey

"The Power for Oneness." is the subject covered in Chapter 13.

■ **Transferable Concepts Books 1–4**   by Dr. Bill Bright.

1. **How to Be Sure You Are a Christian**
2. **How to Experience God's Love and Forgiveness**
3. **How to Be Filled with the Spirit**
4. **How to Walk In the Spirit**

These booklets explain the "how-to's" of consistent, successful Christian living. Excellent for personal enrichment and as gifts for growing Christians.

Learning to live the Christian life is an ongoing process. The following project will aid you in your discovery of the great adventure of daily walking in the power of the Holy Spirit. Building a home that reflects God's character is a matter of choices—choices that are made by faith, trusting that God's Word is true and that He will do what He promises in Scripture.

As a Couple—5–10 Minutes

Share with each other two or three things that really spoke to your needs from Session Six.

Individually—60–90 Minutes

A. We Must Desire to Walk in the Spirit

1. What does Matthew 5:6 teach about a prerequisite for walking in the power of the Holy Spirit?

_____

_____

_____

2. Why is the desire to be Christlike so important?

_____

_____

3. Proverbs 2:1–5 speaks of a commitment and desire for knowing God. List applications to your marriage that you can discern from this passage.

_____

_____

B. We Must Continually Confess Our Sin

1. Sin plagues us in our relationship with God. It alienates us from Him (Proverbs 15:9) and produces "death" (Romans 6:23). Since sin breaks our fellowship with God, it is necessary to restore that relationship when we find that we have been displeasing Him. What does the Bible say to do when fellowship with God has been broken? (1 John 1:5–10)

_____

_____

2. To confess means "to agree with another." We agree with God that our actions or attitudes are wrong. We then repent, turning from these sins and back to God, thanking Him for Christ's death on the cross for all our sins. Why is repentance crucial to our confession?

_____

_____

3. Read Colossians 2:13, 14. When we confess our sin before God, should we:

☐ beg for God's forgiveness?
☐ thank Him that the penalty has been paid and that He has already forgiven us?

NOTE: An exercise that hundreds of thousands of Christians have found meaningful is to take a separate sheet of paper and spend time alone with God, asking Him to reveal any sin that is unconfessed before Him. The following steps are recommended:

1. Title the page, "For God's Eyes Only." Prayerfully list on the page actions and attitudes that are contrary to God's Word and purposes. Focus on areas that affect your mate.

2. After 15–20 minutes, write the words of 1 John 1:9 across your list of sins, thanking God for His absolute forgiveness of all that you have done in the past, present, and future. Thank Him for sending His Son to the cross to die for your sin.

3. It may be necessary and appropriate for you to also confess to your mate any attitudes or actions that have been harmful to him/her. CAUTION: Do not dredge up something from the past that would be more than your mate can handle. Seek wise counsel and avoid dropping any "atomic bombs." There is a significant difference between confessing something that your mate knows about and "getting something off your chest" that makes you feel better but becomes a severe problem to your mate.

4. Destroy the page and continue your study on being filled with the Holy Spirit.

4. When you are tempted to sin, what does God's Word promise in 1 Corinthians 10:13?

_____

_____

5. As a Christian, you have power over sin. Read Romans 6:1–18 and answer the following questions:

a. What happened to your sinful nature when you received Christ? (v. 6)

_____

_____

b. According to verse 11, what must you do?

_____

_____

c. According to verses 16 and 17, what choices must you make?

_____

_____

d. Have you been freed from sin?   ☐ Yes   ☐ No

   Are you still a slave to sin?   ☐ Yes   ☐ No

   To what are you to be a slave?

_____

_____

e. What do you need to do as a result of studying these verses about the freedom Christ has given you?

_____

_____

C. We Must Yield Ownership of Our Life to Jesus Christ

1. What do Romans 6:12–14; 12:1, 2 tell you to do?

_____

_____

2. Have you ever given Jesus Christ complete ownership of your life?   ☐ Yes   ☐ No

If not, would you like to right now?   ☐ Yes   ☐ No

Simply bow in prayer and acknowledge His authority over your life. Give Him the "title deed." Write out your commitment to Him in the space below. Sign and date your statement.

_____

_____

_____

_____

_____

_____

_____

_____

_____

_____

_____   _____

Signature   Date

D. We Must By Faith Claim the Filling of the Holy Spirit

1. Check each statement as you read:

☐ **His Command:** Be filled with the Spirit (Ephesians 5:18).

☐ **His Promise:** He will always answer when we pray according to his will (1 John 5:14, 15).

2. Is it God's will that you be filled with His Spirit?

☐ Yes ☐ No (Review #1 if you are not sure.)

3. When you pray in faith and ask God to fill you, will He do it?

☐ Yes ☐ No

How do you know? (Check #1 again.) _____

4. Why not express right now your obedience and faith to God?

Dear Father, I need you. I admit that I have been directing my own life and I have sinned against you. I thank you that you have forgiven my sins through Christ's death on the cross for me. I now invite Christ to be Lord over all my life. Fill me with the Holy Spirit as you commanded me to be filled, and as you promised in your Word that you would do if I ask in faith. As an expression of my faith, I now thank you for directing my life and for filling me with the Holy Spirit. Amen.

If this prayer expressed the desire of your heart, then simply bow in prayer and trust God to empower you with the Holy Spirit **right now**.

Interact As a Couple—15–20 Minutes

Share with one another the decision you have made in response to this study. Your relationship with one another will benefit as you openly talk about your spiritual commitments—as well as confiding any questions or struggles. Close your time together by praying for one another.

Be ready to share with the group one specific experience from this project: perhaps an instance when you allowed the Holy Spirit to fill you in your marriage relationship—or one area in which you have recognized a struggle in yielding to His control.

Remember to bring your calendar for **Make a Date** to the next session.

The HomeBuilders

C O U P L E S   S E R I E S

"Unless the Lord builds the house,
they labor in vain who build it."
Psalm 127:1

Focus

God's purpose for marriage goes
beyond intimacy, sharing romantic
times together, and achieving oneness.
Marriage is meant to be a couple's
locking arms together to influence
their world and future generations
with the Gospel of Jesus Christ.

We have been exposed to much about God's plan for our marriages so far in our study.

1. Mark the concept that you have found to be most significant in your marriage:

☐ We must deal with the threats to oneness that result in isolation.

☐ We must understand God's blueprints as shown in five purposes for marriage (Mirror, Multiply, Manage, Mutually Complete, Model)

☐ We build a solid foundation by receiving our mate as a gift from God.

☐ We construct according to God's plan when we leave, cleave, and become one flesh, resulting in total transparency with our mate.

☐ We fit together with our mate when we commit to fulfilling our roles defined in the blueprint of Scripture.

☐ We are empowered by the Holy Spirit to carry out these principles and purposes.

2. What do you feel is the most important change you have made thus far in your marriage as a result of this series?

_____

_____

_____

_____

_____

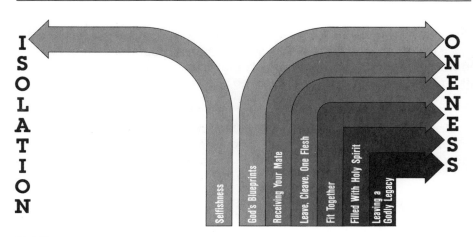

Isolation ← Selfishness, God's Blueprints, Receiving Your Mate, Leave, Cleave, One Flesh, Fit Together, Filled With Holy Spirit, Leaving a Godly Legacy → Oneness

We have learned many things about how to let the Lord build our house. Now we need to learn that "building the house" is not an end in itself.

Although God is deeply interested in our fulfillment as individuals within marriage, He does not give us a "great and satisfying" marriage just so that we can have a warm and wonderful relationship with another person. Scripture teaches that in marriage we are to experience growth and acceptance in order to enable us to reach beyond the doors of our home to a neighborhood and a world in great need.

God's heart of love is virtually breaking over people who have not yet received His forgiveness through His Son Jesus Christ. Reconciling people to Himself is God's desire for every individual and for every marriage. You and your mate and those you influence for Christ, including your children, are all a part of God's purpose for planet Earth.

We have already seen that oneness with God and with our mate is necessary for overcoming isolation in our marriages. The oneness we are establishing in our homes is also enabling us to reach out to others afflicted by isolation.

A couple that is working together to meet needs beyond their own front door will leave a spiritual legacy that will outlive them. In so doing, they will discover that their marriage is thriving as they give their lives away in ministering to the needs of others.

HomeBuilders Principle #10: The heritage you were handed is not as important as the legacy you will leave.

A. Understanding Our Heritage

1. What comes to mind when you think of a "heritage" or a "legacy"?

_____

_____

2. There are other types of legacies which people leave. List as many different kinds as you can.

_____   _____

_____   _____

_____   _____

3. To what extent is the legacy a person leaves a statement of his or her true values? Explain why this would be so.

_____

_____

4. Describe the heritage your parents left to you and the values it represents.

_____

_____

5. Look up the following scriptures and write down words or phrases that describe the legacy God desires you to leave.

Deuteronomy 6:1, 2, 5–7 _____

Joshua 24:14, 15 _____

Psalms 112:1, 2 _____

Proverbs 4:10–15 _____

2 Timothy 1:5 _____

3 John 4 _____

Leaving a godly legacy will ultimately be different for every individual. The true test in leaving a godly legacy is an individual's or a couple's faithful fulfillment of God's mission through the stewardship of time, talents, and treasure. A godly legacy can be partially measured in the character of the descendants who have been spiritually influenced by a person's life.

HomeBuilders Principle #11: The legacy you leave is determined by the life you live.

B. How to Leave a Legacy That Will Outlive You

According to 2 Timothy 2:2 and Psalm 78:3–8, you can leave spiritual as well as physical descendants.

1. How do you leave a spiritual legacy? (Matthew 28:19, 20).

_____

_____

_____

2. According to Deuteronomy 6:4–9, how do you leave a godly legacy through your influence on your children, your physical descendants?

_____

_____

_____

An Example of Leaving a Spiritual Legacy

As you near the completion of this study, you have become part of the godly legacy from a remarkable single woman who left no physical descendants. Humanly speaking, this series might never have been created if it had not been that Dr. Henrietta Mears befriended a young couple in the early years of their spiritual growth. Bill Bright, founder of Campus Crusade for Christ, and his wife Vonette were strongly influenced by Dr. Mears.

Many other individuals and organizations are part of the spiritual legacy left by Dr. Mears, including Billy Graham, Donn Moomaw (President Reagan's pastor at Bel Air Presbyterian Church), Richard

Halverson (Chaplain of the United States Senate), Gospel Light
Publications (a major producer of Bible study resources and Christian
literature), Forest Home (one of the largest Christian conference
centers in the United States), and Gospel Literature International
(GLINT—a service organization aiding in the translation of Christian
literature throughout the world).

If you have grown spiritually through **The HomeBuilders Couples
Series**, then you are a part of the spiritual legacy of Henrietta Mears.
Do you believe that God could still be multiplying **your** spiritual
legacy three generations from now?

> HomeBuilders Principle #12: Your marriage should leave a
> legacy of love that will influence future generations.

C. Motivation for Leaving a Godly Legacy

1. What in the following verses motivates you to leave a godly
legacy?

Matthew 28:19, 20 _____

Romans 1:16 _____

Romans 8:35–39 _____

Ephesians 2:10 _____

1 Peter 3:9–15 _____

2 Peter 3:9–15 _____

2. Read 1 Corinthians 3:10–15 and contrast the final results of a worldly and godly legacy.

_____

_____

3. Describe the legacy you would leave if your life ended tonight:

_____

_____

_____

_____

_____

_____

_____

Construction

(to be completed as a couple)

NOTE: If time does not allow you to complete this section during the session, do so when you **Make a Date**.

1. What do you want your legacy to be? What people do you need to influence for God? What are some tasks in your church you are gifted to tackle? What project should you support?

_____

_____

_____

2. Evaluate the type of legacy your marriage is now leaving in the following areas. Focus on one or two areas.

Love for People _____

Values _____

Schedule and Priorities _____

Sharing Christ with Friends/Associates _____

Finances/Possessions _____

Leadership _____

Children _____

3. What one specific action do you need to take to better use your marriage to leave a godly legacy? Consider:

☐ Commit to participate in other studies of **The HomeBuilders Couples Series**.

☐ Gather another group of couples and lead them in studying **Building Your Marriage**.

☐ Begin weekly family nights—teaching your children about Christ.

☐ Host an Evangelistic Dinner Party—invite your non-Christian friends to your home and as a couple share your faith in Christ and the forgiveness of His gospel.

☐ Share the good news of Jesus Christ with neighborhood children.

☐ _____

_____

For information on any of the above ministry opportunities, contact your local church, or write:

FamilyLife
P.O. Box 23840
Little Rock, AR 72221-3840
(501) 223-8663

4. Most people seek to leave a legacy that will honor them. What does Psalm 45:16, 17 add to this goal? How can you and your mate make this a reality in your marriage and family?

_____

_____

_____

_____

Make a date with your mate this week to complete the last **HomeBuilders Project**.

Date	Time	Location

■

Recommended Reading

■ **Staying Close**   by Dennis Rainey

"A Mother's Influence," "A Word to Dads," "Your Family Can Make the Difference," and "How to Become a HomeBuilder" are recommended chapters for this session.

■ **Dream Big: The Henrietta Mears Story**   edited by Earl Roe

After completing this project, send a **copy** to your group leader within seven to ten days.

Individually—20–30 Minutes

Write out a description of the legacy you desire to leave:

a. to your physical descendants—your children, if God so blesses:

_____

_____

b. to your spiritual descendants—those you lead to Christ and disciple:

_____

_____

Interact As a Couple—20–30 Minutes

1. Compare your descriptions, then make one common description of the legacy you both desire to leave:

a. for your physical descendants

_____

_____

b. for your spiritual descendants

_____

_____

2. Copy or type your statement and place it at work or home as a reminder of your objective. You may want to mount or frame it.

3. Discuss options that are available to you (individually and as a couple) to equip and assist you to leave a godly legacy (local church, Bible study group, outreach event).

_____

_____

4. Write one major objective you wish to accomplish this year in helping you:

a. leave a godly line of physical descendants: _____

_____

_____

b. leave a godly line of spiritual descendants: _____

_____

_____

Where do you go from here?

Conclusion

Where Do You Go from Here?

It is my prayer that you have benefited greatly from this study in **The HomeBuilders Couples Series**. I hope that your marriage will continue to grow as you both submit your lives to Jesus Christ and build according to His blueprints.

I also hope that you will begin reaching out to strengthen other marriages in your community and local church. Your pastor needs lay couples, like yourselves, who are committed to building Christian marriages. One of my favorite World War II stories illustrates this point very clearly.

The year was 1940. The French Army had just collapsed under the siege of Hitler's onslaught. The Dutch had folded, overwhelmed by the Nazi regime. The Belgians had surrendered. And the British Army was trapped on the coast of France in the channel port of Dunkirk.

Two hundred and twenty thousand of Britain's finest young men seemed doomed to die, turning the English Channel red with their blood. The Fuehrer's troops, only miles away in the hills of France, didn't realize how close to victory they actually were.

Any rescue seemed feeble and futile in the time remaining. A "thin" British Navy—"the professionals"—told King George VI that at best they could save 17,000 troops. The House of Commons was warned to prepare for "hard and heavy tidings."

Politicians were paralyzed. The King was powerless. And the allies could only watch as spectators from a distance. Then as the doom of the British Army seemed imminent, a strange fleet appeared on the horizon of the English Channel: the wildest assortment of boats perhaps ever assembled in history. Trawlers, tugs, scows, fishing sloops, lifeboats, pleasure craft, smacks and coasters, sailboats, an island ferry by the name of **Gracie Fields**, even the **Endeavor**, the America's Cup challenger, came, as well

146

as the London fire-brigade flotilla. EACH SHIP WAS MANNED BY CIVILIAN VOLUNTEERS—ENGLISH FATHERS SAILING TO RESCUE BRITAIN'S EXHAUSTED, BLEEDING SONS.

William Manchester writes in his epic novel, **The Last Lion**, that even today what happened in 1940 in less than 24 hours seems like a miracle —not only were all of the British soldiers rescued, but 118,000 Allied troops as well.

Today the Christian home is much like those troops at Dunkirk. Pressured, trapped, and demoralized, it needs help. Your help. The Christian community may be much like England—we stand waiting for politicians, professionals, even for our pastor to step in and save the family. But the problem is much larger than all of those combined can solve.

With the highest divorce rate of any nation on earth, we need an all-out rescue effort by American men and women "sailing" to rescue the exhausted and wounded family casualties. No paid professionals, just common couples with faith in an uncommon God. For too long, those of us in full-time vocational ministry have robbed lay men and women, like you, of the privilege and responsibility of influencing others.

Possibly this study has indeed been used to "light the torch" of your spiritual lives. Perhaps it was already burning and this provided more fuel. Regardless, may we challenge you to invest your lives in others?

You and other couples around the United States can team together to build thousands of marriages and families. By starting a **HomeBuilders** group you will not only strengthen other marriages; you will also see your marriage grow as you teach these principles to others.

Will **you join with us in "Touching Lives . . . Changing Families?"**

147

The following are some practical ways you can make a difference in families today:

1. Gather a group of couples (4–7) and lead them through the seven sessions of this **HomeBuilders** study, **Building Your Marriage**. (Why not consider challenging others in your church or community to form new **HomeBuilders** groups?)

2. Commit to participate in **Building Your Mate's Self-Esteem**, another book in **The HomeBuilders Couples Series**. And continue marriage building with the study book, **Building Teamwork in Marriage**.

4. Show the film, *Jesus*, on video as an evangelistic outreach in your neighborhood. For more information, write to:

        Inspirational Media
        30012 Ivy Glenn Dr., Suite 200
        Laguna Niguel, CA 92677

5. Host an Evangelistic Dinner Party—invite your non-Christian friends to your home and as a couple share your faith in Christ and the forgiveness of His gospel.

6. Share the good news of Jesus Christ with neighborhood children.

7. If you have attended the FamilyLife Marriage Conference, why not assist your pastor in counseling premarrieds using the material you received?

For information on any of the above ministry opportunities, contact your local church, or write:

        FamilyLife
        P.O. Box 23840
        Little Rock, AR 72221-3840
        (501) 223-8663

About the Author:

Dennis Rainey, the author of this study and general editor of **The HomeBuilders Couples Series,** is Director of FamilyLife of Campus Crusade for Christ International. A graduate of the University of Arkansas and Dallas Theological Seminary, he joined the staff of Campus Crusade for Christ International in 1970. Dennis is featured in **The HomeBuilders Film Series** and is author, with his wife, Barbara, of *The Questions Book* and *Building Your Mate's Self-Esteem.* Dennis and Barbara Rainey are the parents of six children—Ashley, Benjamin, Samuel, Rebecca, Deborah, and Laura. They live in Little Rock, Arkansas.

APPENDIX A

The Four Spiritual Laws*

J ust as there are physical laws that govern the physical universe, so are there spiritual laws which govern your relationship with God.

> **LAW ONE: God loves you and offers a wonderful plan for your life.**

God's Love

"For God so loved the world, that He gave His only begotten Son, that whoever believes in Him should not perish, but have eternal life" (John 3:16).

God's Plan

(Christ speaking) "I came that they might have life, and might have it abundantly" (that it might be full and meaningful) (John 10:10).

Why is it that most people are not experiencing the abundant life? Because . . .

> **LAW TWO: Man is sinful and separated from God. Therefore, he cannot know and experience God's love and plan for his life.**

Man Is Sinful

"For all have sinned and fall short of the glory of God" (Romans 3:23).

Man was created to have fellowship with God; but, because of his stubborn self-will, chose to go his own independent way, and

* Written by Bill Bright. Copyright © Campus Crusade for Christ, Inc., 1965, all rights reserved.

fellowship with God was broken. This self-will, characterized by an attitude of active rebellion or passive indifference, is evidence of what the Bible calls sin.

Man Is Separated

"For the wages of sin is death" (spiritual separation from God) (Romans 6:23).

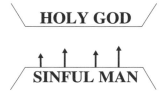

This diagram illustrates that God is holy and man is sinful. A great gulf separates the two. The arrows illustrate that man is continually trying to reach God and the abundant life through his own efforts, such as a good life, philosophy, or religion.

The third law explains the only way to bridge this gulf . . .

> **LAW THREE: Jesus Christ is God's only provision for man's sin. Through Him you can know and experience God's love and plan for your life.**

He Died in Our Place

"But God demonstrates His own love toward us, in that while we were yet sinners, Christ died for us" (Romans 5:8).

He Rose from the Dead

"Christ died for our sins . . . He was buried . . . He was raised on the third day according to the Scriptures . . . He appeared to

[Peter], then to the twelve. After that He appeared to more than five hundred . . ." (1 Corinthians 15:3–6).

He Is the Only Way to God

"Jesus said to him, 'I am the way, and the truth, and the life; no one comes to the Father, but through Me'" (John 14:6).

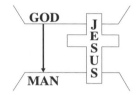

This diagram illustrates that God has bridged the gulf which separates us from Him by sending His Son, Jesus Christ, to die on the cross in our place to pay the penalty for our sins.

It is not enough just to know these three laws . . .

LAW FOUR: We must individually receive Jesus Christ as Savior and Lord; then we can know and experience God's love and plan for our lives.

We Must Receive Christ

"But as many as received Him, to them He gave the right to become children of God, even to those who believe in His name" (John 1:12).

We Receive Christ through Faith

"For by grace you have been saved through faith; and that not of yourselves, it is the gift of God; not as a result of works, that no one should boast" (Ephesians 2:8–9).

When We Receive Christ, We Experience a New Birth

(Read John 3:1–8.)

We Receive Christ by Personal Invitation

(Christ is speaking): "Behold, I stand at the door and knock; if any one hears My voice and opens the door, I will come in to him" (Revelation 3:20).

Receiving Christ involves turning to God from self (repentance) and trusting Christ to come into our lives to forgive our sins and to make us the kind of people He wants us to be. Just to agree intellectually that Jesus Christ is the Son of God and that He died on the cross for our sins is not enough. Nor is it enough to have an emotional experience. We receive Jesus Christ by faith, as an act of the will.

These two circles represent two kinds of lives:

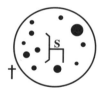

SELF-DIRECTED LIFE

S —Self is on the throne
†—Christ is outside the life
• —Interests are directed by self, often resulting in discord and frustration

CHRIST-DIRECTED LIFE

†—Christ is in the life and on the throne
S —Self is yielding to Christ
• —Interests are directed by Christ, resulting in harmony with God's plan

Which circle best represents your life?

Which circle would you like to have represent your life?

You Can Receive Christ Right Now by Faith through Prayer

(Prayer is talking with God.)

God knows your heart and is not so concerned with your words as He is with the attitude of your heart. The following is a suggested prayer:

> "Lord Jesus, I need You. Thank You for dying on the cross for my sins. I open the door of my life and receive You as my Savior and Lord. Thank You for forgiving my sins and giving me eternal life. Make me the kind of person You want me to be."

Does this prayer express the desire of your heart?

If it does, pray this prayer right now, and Christ will come into your life, as He promised.

APPENDIX B

Have You Made the Wonderful Discovery
of the Spirit-Filled Life?*

E very day can be an exciting adventure for the Christian who knows the reality of being filled with the Holy Spirit and who lives constantly, moment by moment, under His gracious control.

T he Bible tells us that there are three kinds of people:

1. NATURAL MAN (one who has not received Christ)

"But a natural man does not accept the things of the Spirit of God; for they are foolishness to him, and he cannot understand them, because they are spiritually appraised" (1 Corinthians 2:14).

SELF-DIRECTED LIFE

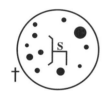

S —Ego or finite self is on the throne
†—Christ is outside the life
• —Interests are controlled by self, often resulting
   in discord and frustration

2. SPIRITUAL MAN (one who is controlled and empowered by the Holy Spirit)

"But he who is spiritual appraises all things . . ." (1 Corinthians 2:15).

CHRIST-DIRECTED LIFE

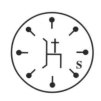

†—Christ is on the throne of the life
S —Ego or self is dethroned
• —Interests are under control of infinite God,
   resulting in harmony with God's plan

3. CARNAL MAN (one who has received Christ, but who lives in defeat because he trusts in his own efforts to live the Christian life)

SELF-DIRECTED LIFE

E—Ego or finite self is on the throne
†—Christ is dethroned
•—Interests are controlled by self, often resulting in discord and frustration

"And I, brethren, could not speak to you as to spiritual men, but as to carnal men, as to babes in Christ. I gave you milk to drink, not solid food; for you were not yet able to receive it. Indeed, even now you are not yet able, for you are still carnal. For since there is jealousy and strife among you, are you not fleshly, and are you not walking like mere men?" (1 Corinthians 3:1–3).

A. God has Provided for Us an Abundant and Fruitful Christian Life.

Jesus said, "I came that they might have life, and might have it abundantly" (John 10:10).

"I am the vine, you are the branches; he who abides in Me, and I in him, he bears much fruit; for apart from Me you can do nothing" (John 15:5).

"But the fruit of the Spirit is love, joy, peace, patience, kindness, goodness, faithfulness, gentleness, self-control; against such things there is no law" (Galatians 5:22, 23).

"But you shall receive power when the Holy Spirit has come upon you; and you shall be My witnesses both in Jerusalem, and in all Judea and Samaria, and even to the remotest part of the earth" (Acts 1:8).

THE SPIRITUAL MAN

Some Personal Traits Which Result from Trusting God:

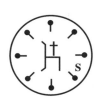

Christ-centered
Empowered by the Holy Spirit
Introduces others to Christ
Effective prayer life
Understands God's Word
Trusts God
Obeys God

Love
Joy
Peace
Patience
Kindness
Goodness
Faithfulness

The degree to which these traits are manifested in the life depends upon the extent to which the Christian trusts the Lord with every detail of his life, and upon his maturity in Christ. One who is only beginning to understand the ministry of the Holy Spirit should not be discouraged if he is not as fruitful as more mature Christians who have known and experienced this truth for a longer period.

Why is it that most Christians are not experiencing the abundant life?

B. Carnal Christians Cannot Experience the Abundant and Fruitful Christian Life.

The carnal man trusts in his own efforts to live the Christian life:

1. He is either uninformed about, or has forgotten, God's love, forgiveness, and power (Romans 5:8–10; Hebrews 10:1–25; 1 John 1; 2:1–3; 2 Peter 1:9; Acts 1:8).

2. He has an up-and-down spiritual experience.

3. He cannot understand himself—he wants to do what is right, but cannot.

4. He fails to draw upon the power of the Holy Spirit to live the Christian life.

(1 Corinthians 3:1–3; Romans 7:15–24; 8:7; Galatians 5:16–18)

THE CARNAL MAN

Some or all of the following traits may characterize the Christian who does not fully trust God:

Ignorance of his
   spiritual heritage
Unbelief
Disobedience
Loss of love for God and
   for others
Poor prayer life
No desire for Bible study

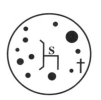

Legalistic attitude
Discouragement
Impure thoughts
Jealousy
Guilt
Critical spirit
Worry
Frustration
Aimlessness

(The individual who professes to be a Christian but who continues to practice sin should realize that he may not be a Christian at all, according to 1 John 2:3; 3:6–9; Ephesians 5:5.)

The third truth gives us the only solution to this problem . . .

C. Jesus Promised the Abundant and Fruitful Life as the Result of Being Filled (Controlled and Empowered) by the Holy Spirit.

The Spirit-filled life is the Christ-controlled life, by which Christ lives His life in and through us in the power of the Holy Spirit (John 15).

1. One becomes a Christian through the ministry of the Holy Spirit, according to John 3:1–8. From the moment of spiritual birth, the Christian is indwelt by the Holy Spirit at all times (John 1:12; Colossians 2:9–10; John 14:16–17). Though all Christians are indwelt by the Holy Spirit, not all Christians are filled (controlled and empowered) by the Holy Spirit.

2. The Holy Spirit is the source of the overflowing life (John 7:37–39).

3. The Holy Spirit came to glorify Christ (John 16:1–5). When one is filled with the Holy Spirit, he is a true disciple of Christ.

4. In His last command before His ascension, Christ promised the power of the Holy Spirit to enable us to be witnesses for Him (Acts 1:1–9).

How, then, can one be filled with the Holy Spirit?

D. We Are Filled (Controlled and Empowered) by the Holy Spirit by Faith; Then We Can Experience the Abundant and Fruitful Life Which Christ Promised to Each Christian.

You can appropriate the filling of the Holy Spirit *right now* if you:

1. Sincerely desire to be controlled and empowered by the Holy Spirit (Matthew 5:6; John 7:37–39).

2. Confess your sins.

By faith thank God that He has forgiven all of your sins—past, present, and future—because Christ died for you (Colossians 2:13–15; 1 John 1; 2:1–3; Hebrews 10:1–17).

3. By faith claim the fullness of the Holy Spirit, according to:

a. HIS COMMAND—Be filled with the Spirit. "And do not get drunk with wine, for that is dissipation, but be filled with the Spirit" (Ephesians 5:18).

b. HIS PROMISE—He will always answer when we pray according to His will. "And this is the confidence which we have before Him, that, if we ask anything according to His will, He hears us. And if we know that He hears us in whatever we ask, we know that we have the requests which we have asked from Him" (1 John 5:14–15).

Faith can be expressed through prayer . . .

161

How to Pray in Faith to Be Filled with the Holy Spirit

We are filled with the Holy Spirit by *faith* alone. However, true prayer is one way of expressing your faith. The following is a suggested prayer:

> *"Dear Father, I need You. I acknowledge that I have been in control of my life; and that, as a result, I have sinned against You. I thank You that You have forgiven my sins through Christ's death on the cross for me. I now invite Christ to again take control of the throne of my life. Fill me with the Holy Spirit as You commanded me to be filled, and as You promised in your Word that You would do if I asked in faith. I pray this in the name of Jesus. As an expression of my faith, I now thank You for taking control of my life and for filling me with the Holy Spirit."*

Does this prayer express the desire of your heart? If so, bow in prayer and trust God to fill you with the Holy Spirit right now.

How to Know that You are Filled (Controlled and Empowered) by the Holy Spirit

Did you ask God to fill you with the Holy Spirit? Do you know that you are now filled with the Holy Spirit? On what authority? (On the trustworthiness of God Himself and His Word: Hebrews 11:6; Romans 14:22–23).

Do not depend upon feelings. The promise of God's Word, not our feelings, is our authority. The Christian lives by faith (trust) in the trustworthiness of God Himself and His Word. This train diagram illustrates the relationship between **fact** (God and His Word), **faith** (our trust in God and His Word), and **feeling** (the result of our faith and obedience) (John 14:21).

The train will run with or without the caboose. However, it would be futile to attempt to pull the train by the caboose. In the same way, we, as Christians, do not depend upon feelings or emotions, but we place our faith (trust) in the trustworthiness of God and the promises of His Word.

How to Walk in the Spirit

Faith (trust in God and His promises) is the only means by which a Christian can live the Spirit-controlled life. As you continue to trust Christ moment by moment:

1. Your life will demonstrate more and more of the fruit of the Spirit (Galatians 5:22–23); and will be more and more conformed to the image of Christ (Romans 12:2; 2 Corinthians 3:18).

2. Your prayer life and study of God's Word will become more meaningful.

3. You will experience His power in witnessing (Acts 1:8).

4. You will be prepared for spiritual conflict against the world (1 John 2:15–17); against the flesh (Galatians 5:16–17); and against Satan (1 Peter 5:7–9; Ephesians 6:10–13).

5. You will experience His power to resist temptation and sin (1 Corinthians 10:13; Philippians 4:13; Ephesians 1:19–23; 6:10; 2 Timothy 1:7; Romans 6;1–16).

Spiritual Breathing

By faith you can continue to experience God's love and forgiveness.

If you become aware of an area of your life (an attitude or an action) that is displeasing to the Lord, even though you are walking with Him and sincerely desiring to serve Him, simply thank God that

He has forgiven your sins—past, present and future—on the basis of Christ's death on the cross. Claim His love and forgiveness by faith and continue to have fellowship with Him.

If you retake the throne of your life through sin—a definite act of disobedience—breathe spiritually.

Spiritual Breathing (exhaling the impure and inhaling the pure) is an exercise in faith that enables you to continue to experience God's love and forgiveness.

1. EXHALE—confess your sin—agree with God concerning your sin and thank Him for His forgiveness of it, according to 1 John 1:9 and Hebrews 10:1–25. Confession involves repentance—a change in attitude and action.

2. INHALE—surrender the control of your life to Christ, and appropriate (receive) the fullness of the Holy Spirit by faith. Trust that He now controls and empowers you, according to the *command* of Ephesians 5:18 and the *promise* of 1 John 5:14–15.

Renew Your Commitment.

Y ou've been working on the most important commitment of your life—spending time with God and with your spouse. No doubt you've learned a lot of things about your mate that will help the two of you grow closer together for years to come. You've also learned a lot about

God's Word and how much it means to study the Bible with each other. But don't let it stop here—lay the next block in the foundation of your marriage by beginning the HomeBuilders Couples Series®. It will help you keep your marriage as strong, as dynamic, as solid as the day you said "I do."

Building Your Marriage
By Dennis Rainey
Help couples get closer together than you ever imagined possible.
•Leader's Guide
ISBN 08307.16130
•Study Guide
ISBN 08307.16122

Building Your Mate's Self-Esteem
By Dennis & Barbara Rainey
Marriage is God's workshop for self-esteem.
•Leader's Guide
ISBN 08307.16173
•Study Guide
ISBN 08307.16165

Building Teamwork in Your Marriage
By Robert Lewis
Help couples celebrate and enjoy their differences
•Leader's Guide
ISBN 08307.16157
•Study Guide
ISBN 08307.16149

Resolving Conflict in Your Marriage
By Bob & Jan Horner
Turn conflict into love and understanding.
•Leader's Guide
ISBN 08307.16203
•Study Guide
ISBN 08307.16181

Mastering Money in Your Marriage
By Ron Blue
Put an end to conflicts and find out how to use money to glorify God.
•Leader's Guide
ISBN 08307.16254
•Study Guide
ISBN 08307.16246

Growing Together In Christ
By David Sunde
Discover how Christ is central to your marriage.
•Leader's Guide
ISBN 08307.16297
•Study Guide
ISBN 08307.16289

Life Choices for a Lasting Marriage
By David Boehi
Find out how to make the right choices in your marriage.
•Leader's Guide
ISBN 08307.16262
•Study Guide
ISBN 08307.16270

Managing Pressure in Your Marriage
By Dennis Rainey & Robert Lewis
Learn how obedience to God will take pressure off your marriage
•Leader's Guide
ISBN 08307.16319
•Study Guide
ISBN 08307.16300

Expressing Love in Your Marriage
By Jerry & Sheryl Wunder and Dennis & Jill Eenigenburg
Discover God's plan for your love life by seeking God's best for your mate.
•Leader's Guide
ISBN 08307.16661
•Study Guide
ISBN 08307.16688

FAMILYLIFE

Look for the **HomeBuilders** Couples Series® at your local Christian bookstore.

Gospel Light

"A Weekend to Remember"

Every couple has a unique set of needs. The FamilyLife Marriage Conference meets couples' needs by equipping them with proven solutions that address practically every component of "How to Build a Better Marriage." The conference gives you the opportunity to slow down and focus on your spouse and your relationship. You will spend an insightful weekend together, doing fun couples' projects and hearing from dynamic speakers on real-life solutions for building and enhancing oneness in your marriage.

You'll learn:

◆ *Five secrets of successful marriage*
◆ *How to implement oneness in your marriage*
◆ *How to maintain a vital sexual relationship*
◆ *How to handle conflict*
◆ *How to express forgiveness to one another*

Our insightful speaker teams also conduct sessions for:

◆ *Soon-to-be-marrieds*
◆ *Men-only*
◆ *Women-only*

The FamilyLife Marriage Conference

To register or receive a free brochure and schedule, call
FamilyLife at 1-800-333-1433.

FAMILYLIFE

A ministry of Campus Crusade for Christ International

Take a Weekend...to Raise Your Children for a Lifetime

Good parents aren't just born that way; they begin with a strong, biblical foundation and then work at improving their parenting skills. That's where we come in.

In one weekend the FamilyLife Parenting Conference will equip you with the principles and tools you need to be more effective parents for a lifetime. Whether you're just getting started or in the turbulent years of adolescence, we'll show you the biblical blueprints for raising your children. You'll hear from dynamic speakers and do fun parenting skills projects designed to help you apply what you've learned. You'll receive proven, effective principles from parents just like you who have dedicated their lives to helping families.

You'll learn how to:

- ◆ *Build a strong relationship with your child*
- ◆ *Help your child develop emotional, spiritual and sexual identity*
- ◆ *Develop moral character in your child*
- ◆ *Give your child a sense of mission*
- ◆ *Pass on your values to your child*

The FamilyLife Parenting Conference

To register or receive a free brochure and schedule, call
FamilyLife at 1-800-333-1433.

FAMILYLIFE

A ministry of Campus Crusade for Christ International

FamilyLife Resources

Building Your Mate's Self-Esteem

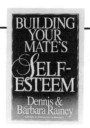

The key to a joy-filled marriage is a strong sense of self-worth in both partners. This practical, best-selling book helps you tap into God's formula for building up your mate. How to overcome problems from the past, how to help your mate conquer self-doubt, how to boost communication, and much more. Creative "Esteem-Builder Projects" will bring immediate results, making your marriage all it can be. The #1 best-seller at FamilyLife Marriage Conferences across America. **Paperback, $8.95**

Pulling Weeds, Planting Seeds

Thirty-eight insightful, thought-provoking chapters, laced with humor, show how you can apply the wisdom of God's Word to your life and home. Includes chapters on making your time with your family count, dealing with tough situations at home and at work, living a life of no regrets, and MUCH MORE. These bite-sized, fun-to-read chapters make this great book hard to put down. **Hardcover, $12.95**

Staying Close

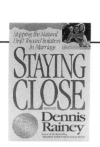

Overcome the isolation that creeps into so many marriages, and watch your marriage blossom! This best-selling book, winner of the 1990 Gold Medallion Award for best book on marriage and family, is packed with practical ideas and HomeBuilders projects to help you experience the oneness God designed for your marriage. How to manage stress. How to handle conflict. How to be a great lover. And much more! Based on 15 years of research and favorite content from the FamilyLife Marriage Conference. **Paperback, $10.95**

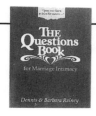

The Questions Book

Discover the miracle of truly understanding each other. This book will lead you into deeper intimacy and joy by giving you 31 sets of fun, thought-provoking questions you can explore and answer together. Space is provided for you to write your answers. Share your innermost feelings, thoughts, goals, and dreams. This book could lead to the best times you'll ever spend together. **Hardcover, $9.95**

For more information on these and other FamilyLife Resources contact your local Christian retailer or call FamilyLife at 1-800-333-1433.

The HomeBuilders

C O U P L E S   S E R I E S

"Unless the Lord builds the house,
they labor in vain who build it."
Psalm 127:1

BYM

HomeBuilders Evaluation

Your First Name _____ Last Name _____

Spouse's First Name _____ Wedding Date _____ Your Age _____

Home Phone _____ Work Phone _____

Address _____

City _____ State _____ ZIP Code _____

Full Church Name _____   May we quote you?
                                                ❑ Yes   ❑ No
Church City _____ State _____

How would you rate this HomeBuilders Couples study?

	Poor							Excellent		
Overall experience	1	2	3	4	5	6	7	8	9	10
Study Guide	1	2	3	4	5	6	7	8	9	10

How many HomeBuilders Couples Series have you now participated in ? [   ]
Describe the effect this HomeBuilders study has had on you and your family:

How would you change or improve this HomeBuilders study?

Would you be willing to lead a separate HomeBuilders study yourself?
     ❑ Yes   ❑ No   ❑ Yes, with more training

Have you attended a FamilyLife Conference? ❑ Yes ❑ No

FamilyLife has many other resources for you and your family. Please check if you would like to receive additional information on the following resources:
❑ Other HomeBuilders Couples Series studies
❑ FamilyLife Marriage Conference
❑ FamilyLife Parenting Conference
❑ "FamilyLife Today" radio program
❑ Books, videos and tapes